Jamie Cullum
Catching Tales

© 2005 BY INTERNATIONAL MUSIC PUBLICATIONS LTD
FIRST PUBLISHED IN 2005 BY INTERNATIONAL MUSIC PUBLICATIONS LTD
INTERNATIONAL MUSIC PUBLICATIONS LTD IS A FABER MUSIC COMPANY
3 QUEEN SQUARE
LONDON
WC1N 3AU

DESIGN BY BARNBROOK DESIGN
PHOTOGRAPHY BY MYRIAM SANTOS—KAYDA

MUSIC ARRANGED BY CHRIS BARON, PAUL HONEY, RICHARD HARRIS & ANDY VINTER
MUSIC PROCESSED BY CAMDEN MUSIC
EDITED BY LUCY HOLLIDAY & MATT GATES
PRINTED IN ENGLAND BY CALIGRAVING LTD
ALL RIGHTS RESERVED

ISBN 0-571-5247-1

TO BUY FABER MUSIC PUBLICATIONS OR TO FIND OUT ABOUT THE FULL RANGE OF TITLES
AVAILABLE, PLEASE CONTACT YOUR LOCAL MUSIC RETAILER OR FABER MUSIC SALES ENQUIRIES:
FABER MUSIC LTD, BURNT MILL, ELIZABETH WAY, HARLOW, CM20 2HX ENGLAND
TEL: +44 (0) 1279 82 89 82
FAX: +44 (0) 1279 82 89 83
SALES@FABERMUSIC.COM
FABERMUSIC.COM

GET YOUR WAY

WORDS AND MUSIC BY JAMIE CULLUM, ALLEN TOUSSAINT AND DANIEL MAKAMURA

1. Dinn-er at eight that sounds fine I s'pose I need to turn up 'round nine,
2. Try to pick it up, reading the signs it's turn-ing out to be a real good time, so

bought a bunch of flow-ers just for her, she says the bur-den's on the re-cei-ver. I
who'd have thought that enter-tain-ment, lies in the wa-ter of your dis-con-tent. Now we

cont. sim.

op - en the door___ and you walked in,   (sniff) the scent of wild Jas - mine.   The
sit at the ta - ble___ face to face,   Queen takes pawn check on check mate.   I

room___ seemed to freeze in time,   my reg - u - lar ta - ble will be just fine.
feel your foot brush against my leg,   I'm not that eas - i - ly led...

Ra - di - ant and el - e - gant you might be,___ but your con - cen - tra - tion is so go light - ly.
You flutter your eyes___ and you toss your hair,   I have to say that it is kinda un - fair.   So

Both of ya eyes___ re - flect the moon,   you real - ly think you own the room.)
let me tell you baby now what's in store,   you'll win the battle but I'll win the war.)

3. This has been fun, I sup - pose al - though my feel - ings are all jux - ta - posed, but

D.S. al Coda

truth be told__ I'm as fic - kle as hell, but gen - tle - men nev - er kiss and tell.

Coda

C#m7

repeat to fade

9

LONDON SKIES

WORDS AND MUSIC BY GUY CHAMBERS AND JAMIE CULLUM

Shapes and cool light wan-der the streets like an ar-my of

strays, on a cold win-ter's day.

Will you let me ro-man-ti - cise

the beau-ty in the Lon-don skies.

You know the sun-light al-ways shines_____

be-hind the clouds____ of Lon-don skies.____

2. Pa-tient____ mo-ments____ chilled to____ the bone____ un-der in-fi-nite greys.

Vis-ion____ hin-dered____ mist set-t'ling low____ like a ghost-ly bal-

the Lon-don skies. You know the sun-light al-ways

shines be-hind the clouds of Lon-don skies.

PHOTOGRAPH

WORDS AND MUSIC BY JAMIE CULLUM

1. Her name was writ-ten on the pho-to-graph,
3. And there's the first time that I tried that stuff,

right next to her red sun-burned face.
I think I look a lit-tle green.

It all had hap-pened in that long
I re-mem-ber throw-ing up be-hind

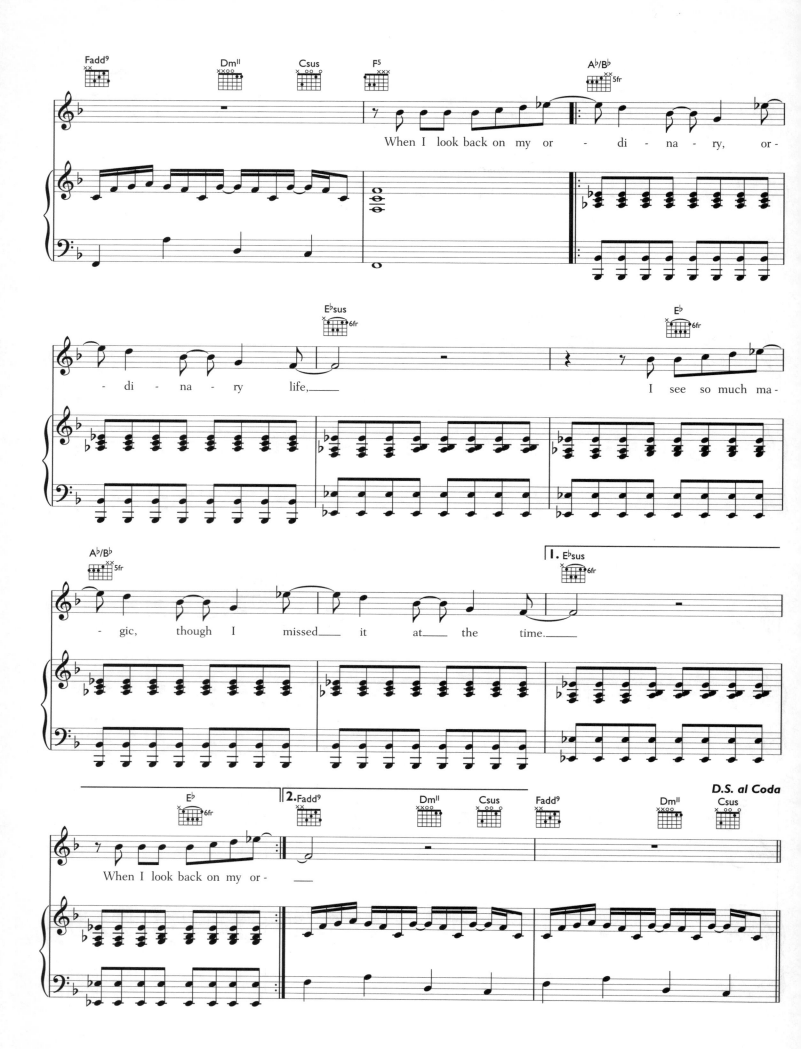

When I look back on my or - di - na - ry, or -

di - na - ry life, I see so much ma -

- gic, though I missed it at the time.

When I look back on my or -

When I look back on my or -

I ONLY HAVE EYES FOR YOU

WORDS BY AL DUBIN AND MUSIC BY HARRY WARREN

Are the stars _____ out to-night? I don't know if it's cloud-y or bright, cos I on - ly have eyes _____ for you dear.

My love must be_____ some kind of blind love, I don't see an-y-

-bo-dy__ but you.__

The moon_____ may_____ be high,_____ but I can't see a thing in the

NOTHING I DO

WORDS AND MUSIC BY JAMIE CULLUM

Swing ♩ = 150

1. We were so drunk last night, we had that
2. Next day I called you back, and you called me a

stu - pid fight___ you called me a use - less, sel - fish prick.___
stu - pid twat,___ then___ you were cry - ing on___ the phone.___

So I'm in a fix___ right now,___ and we'll meas-ure the truth___
You sound-ed___ so___ up - set... you said I was - n't the man___

All to-geth-er now,   1,   2,   3.

(whistle)

repeat to fade

MIND TRICK

WORDS AND MUSIC BY JAMIE CULLUM AND BEN CULLUM

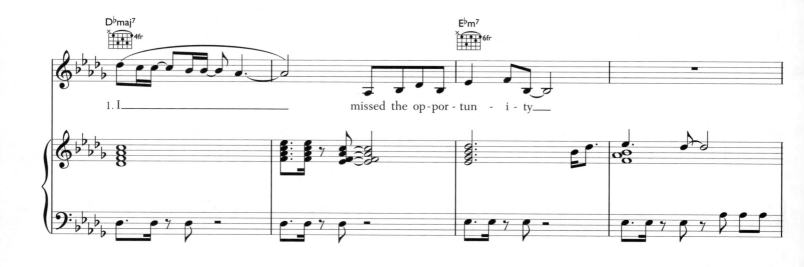

Fall - ing out,____ mak - ing up it seems such___ a sil - ly game___

____ why do I____ nev - er gain?____ If there's mus -

D.S. al Coda I

Coda I

Na na na____ na na na____ na na na____ na na___ na na na

cont. sim.

21ST CENTURY KID

WORDS AND MUSIC BY JAMIE CULLUM

I'M GLAD THERE IS YOU

WORDS AND MUSIC BY JIMMY DORSEY AND PAUL MADEIRA

OH GOD

WORDS AND MUSIC BY GUY CHAMBERS AND JAMIE CULLUM

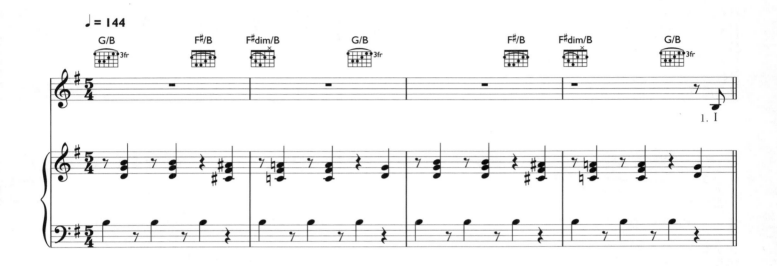

know it's been a while   since I   have talked to you.   But

may - be you're the one   who makes   the   winds   blow.___

Look-ing at the stars with-out ex-pla-na-tion we con-temp-late as kings and sim - - ple men on trial, lit-tle world's fra-gile. Oh God can you tell us when it's going to stop? May-be it's not just

searing rains as our powers interchange.

(Sax. solo)

Oh _____ God can you tell us when it's going to stop?

CATCH THE SUN

WORDS AND MUSIC BY JIMI GOODWIN, JEZ WILLIAMS AND ANDY WILLIAMS

1. Ev - 'ry day_ it_ comes_ to_ this, catch the things you_ might_ have_ missed you say_

— get back to yes - ter - day._

7 DAYS TO CHANGE YOUR LIFE

WORDS AND MUSIC BY JAMIE CULLUM

2. I know some-times your life is a

bitch,

so come pur-chase my___ ea-sy___ fix.___ I've been there my-self,

sad,___ fat and bald, but soon with my help, you'll___ have it all.___

D.S. al Coda

op - ened up the blinds to let the light in on my sor - ry life, I dreamed a - bout suc - cess and mon - ey

mus - cles, wom - en, cars and ev - en wives, and they would al - ways tend to my ev - 'ry need.___

So do you see what you can be, ba - by when you're with

me?_____ In just sev - en short days, you'll change___ your

life._____ All of your inn-o-cence found,_____ you'll ev-en

lose a few___ pounds,___ see your-self mak - ing a mint, qua - li - ty

time___ with your___ kids. Send me your mon-ey,___ and I'll change_____ your

life.

OUR DAY WILL COME

WORDS AND MUSIC BY MORT GARSON AND BOB HILLIARD

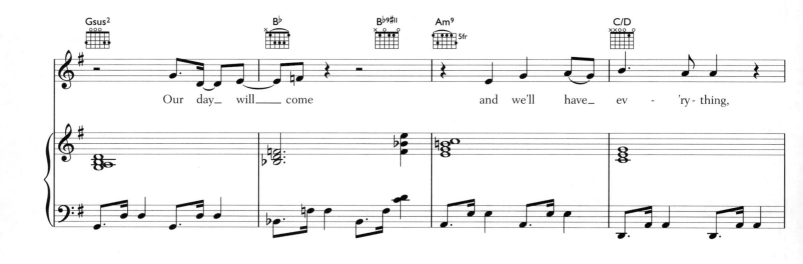

Our day__ will__ come and we'll have__ ev - 'ry - thing,

we'll share the__ joy fall - ing in__ love__ can bring.

And our_ dreams have ma - gic be - cause we'll al - ways stay_____ in_ love_ this way,_

our_ day_____ will____ come.

♩ = ♩ **Double time swing**

Our day,_____ our day,_____ our day____

will____ come.

BACK TO THE GROUND

WORDS AND MUSIC BY JAMIE CULLUM AND ED HARCOURT

3. So clear-ly,   I've let my-self go.

FASCINATING RHYTHM

MUSIC AND LYRICS BY GEORGE GERSHWIN AND IRA GERSHWIN

Doo doo doo doo da da doo doo doo doo dap, doo doo doo doo da da doo doo doo

doo dom. Doo doo doo doo da da doo doo doo doo da doo doo doo doo da da doo doo doo

doo dum. Doo doo doo doo doo doo ba da doo.___

Doo dum dum de bip doo doo doo oh. Wooh. Doo doo doo doo da da, doo

doo doo doo dap, doo doo doo doo da da doo doo doo doo dum. Doo doo doo doo da da doo

doo doo doo be doo doo doo doo doo da da doo doo doo doo dum. Doo doo doo

doo da da da da da da da doo doo.___ Doo doo doo doo da da doo

doo doo doo da di doo. Doo doo doo doo dum doo. Doo doo doo doo doo

damp piano strings
with hands

doo.

3   3

Ba

N.C.

bom da da da dum da da, ba bom da da da dum ba da da dum. Ba bom da ba da da

da da,   ba bom da   da da dum da da da   da da.

Fas - ci - nat - ing rhy - thm,   you got me on the go,   fas - ci - nat - ing rhy - thm,   I'm all a   qui - ver.

What a mess you're mak-ing, the neigh-bours want to know why I'm al-ways shak-ing just like my

grand-mo- ther. Each morn - ing I get up with the sun,___

to find at___ night no work___ has been done...

I know that once it did-n't mat-ter, but now you do-ing wrong, when you start to pat-ter I'm so un-

hap-py. Won't you take a day off, de-cide to run a-long, some-where far a-way off, and make it

snap-py. Oh how I long to be___ the man___ I used___ to be,___

___ fas-ci-nat-ing rhy-thm, why don't you stop pick-ing on me.

Huh. Ba bom ba da da dum ba da, ba bom da da da dum

za da da doom, ba bom da da da dum da da, doo

doo doo doo doo doo da da da uh doo doo doo doo doo doo da da da doo doo

doo doo doo doo doo da dap, doo doo doo doo doo doo da da da doo, doo

doo doo doo doo doo da da, ba doo doo doo doo doo da da da doo.

hands on piano lid

MY YARD

WORDS AND MUSIC BY JAMIE CULLUM, BEN CULLUM AND TERON BEAL

1. So hail a ta - xi cab and come a-round here

and I will meet you right out - side

grass is green - er on___ the oth - er side?___ Take a trip to my yard,___

___ oh,___ don't you know the love that you've been dream - ing of___ is mine?

Take a trip to my___ yard,___

don't you know the grass is green - er on___ the oth - er side?___

Take a trip to my yard_____ oh,___ don't you know the

love that you've been dream - ing of___ is mine?___ Take a trip to

my_____ yard.___